RACIAL JUSTICE IN AMERICA
TOPICS for CHANGE

BY

HEDREICH NICHOLS · LEIGH ANN ERICKSON · KELISA WING

No one is born a racist. Racism is taught, and anything that is taught can be unlearned. *Racial Justice in America: Topics for Change* seeks to show that we are better when we are united together. Through awareness and education, learn about the roles you can play in dismantling disparate systems that keep us divided and be empowered to take action wherever injustice exists.

Being anti-racist is not only hard work, but it takes heart work! We know that through education, love, and awareness, we can change this world for the better. It is not too early to begin to learn how to undo systems of oppression and rebuild an equitable system on a foundation of trust, listening, and a desire to create a better world.

We hope this book will create a safe entry point for you to start to have courageous conversations, give you a safe and brave space for learning, and allow you to see yourself as an agent of change in creating racial, social, and emotional justice for all!

–Kelisa Wing

SLEEPING BEAR PRESS™

2395 South Huron Parkway, Suite 200
Ann Arbor, MI 48104
www.sleepingbearpress.com

Printed and bound in the United States.

10 9 8 7 6 5 4 3 2 1

Library of Congress Cataloging-in-Publication Data

Names: Wing, Kelisa, author. | Nichols, Hedreich, author. | Erickson, Leigh Ann, author.
Title: Racial justice in America : topics for change / Kelisa Wing, Hedreich Nichols, Leigh Ann Erickson.
Description: Ann Arbor : Sleeping Bear Press, 2021 | Series: [SBP learning] |
Series statement provided by publisher. | Audience: Ages 10-14 |
Summary: "Topics on race have been avoided in education for too long—allowing racist systems
to continue to thrive. This book explores current questions around race in comprehensive, honest,
and age-appropriate ways. Developed to reach children of all races and encourage them to
approach race issues with open eyes and minds"—Provided by publisher.
Identifiers: LCCN 2020051703 | ISBN 9781534186781 (hardcover)
Subjects: LCSH: Anti-racism—United States—Juvenile literature. | Racism—United States—
Juvenile literature. | Black lives matter movement—Juvenile literature.
| United States—Race relations—Juvenile literature.
Classification: LCC E184.A1 W517 2021 | DDC 305.800973—dc23
LC record available at https://lccn.loc.gov/2020051703

Reading Adviser: Marla Conn, MS, Ed., Literacy specialist, Read-Ability, Inc. | Content Adviser: Kelisa Wing | Book Design/Cover Art: Felicia Macheske

Photo Credits: © Daisy Daisy/Shutterstock, 5; © vasara/Shutterstock, 7; Photograph by Edward S. Curtis, LOC Control No: 94504691; © Library of
Congress/Photograph by William R. Howell, LOC Control No.: 2016652289; 11; Library of Congress/Photograph by Arthur Rothstein, LOC Control No.:
2017777149, 11; © Xackery Irving/Shutterstock, 13; Dee Dalasio/Shutterstock, 14; © Motortion Films/Shutterstock, 15; © FS Stock/Shutterstock, 19;
© VGstockstudio/Shutterstock, 20; Library of Congress/Photograph by Warren Leffler, LOC Control No.: 2003673955, 23; Library of Congress/LOC
Control No.: 2007676238, 25; Library of Congress/Photograph by Thomas J. O'Halloran, LOC Control No.: 2003654384, 27; © Hong Chung Chih/
Shutterstock, 28; © Monkey Business Images/Shutterstock, 29; © Rawpixel/Shutterstock, 30-31; © Pova1964/Shutterstock, 33; © Iris Basile/
Shutterstock, 35; © Rena Schild/Shutterstock, 36; © lev radin/Shutterstock, 37; Library of Congress/Photograph by Russell Lee, LOC Control No.:
2017740552, 39; Library of Congress/LOC Control No.: 2017629761, 40; Library of Congress/LOC Control No.: 2007664440, 40; © ADUC/Shutterstock, 41;
© Allison C Bailey/Shutterstock, 44; © Aadley C Bullock/Shutterstock, 45; © Karl Tapales/Shutterstock, 46; Cultura Motion/Shutterstock, 47

Graphics Throughout: © debra hughes/Shutterstock; © GoodStudio/Shutterstock; © Natewimon Nantiwat/Shutterstock; © Galyna_P/Shutterstock;
© artishock/Shutterstock

Table of
CONTENTS

What Is ANTI-RACISM?

THE BASICS

Being treated badly because of the way you look isn't fair. And bullying someone because of their skin color or how they identify is wrong. That's what racism is—treating someone badly because of their skin color, culture, or identity. Mostly, no one wants to be racist. But what does being anti-racist mean? Isn't that the same as *not* being racist? If not being racist isn't enough, what else is there?

These are the kinds of questions you might think of when you hear the word *anti-racism* for the first time. The good thing is, if you aren't treating others differently because of the way they look, you're already on your way to becoming anti-racist. Being anti-racist begins with not being racist, but it goes beyond that. It means that you identify with *being something* rather than being *not* something.

For example, you can be an actor or not an actor. OR, you can be an actor *or* a gamer; an actor *or* a basketball player; an actor *or* a writer; an actor *or* a scientist . . . Get the idea? If all you are is *not* an actor, you're just there, not really doing anything at all. But, if you are working at being something other than an actor, you identify with behaviors, skills, talents, and a community of people who are doing the same thing. You are actively involved, playing, writing a book, or winning a science fair; you are being something rather than *not* being something.

Being anti-racist means you are *not* being racist. But it also means you are actively helping to make sure that racism becomes less of a problem—until it hardly exists at all.

Black people in America face racism in schools, in their communities, and in the workplace.

Where Did "RACE" Come From?

There are quite a few theories about where the word race came from. Some say it came from the French language between the 14th and 17th centuries. Others say it's an Italian or Hebrew word. But all agree that there are no races of humans. We are all categorized as Homo sapiens. And traits like skin, eye, and hair pigmentation don't change that.

Differences in skin color have evolved over time based on the needs of humans living in different climates. The substance responsible for skin color is called melanin, and it also protects the skin from sunburn and skin cancer.

Originally, people living near the equator developed more melanin and darker skin to help protect them from the sun. As people migrated farther north, many thousands of years ago, their skin began to adapt to colder climates where less protection from the sun was needed. As their need for melanin decreased, their bodies began to produce less of it. This is why the farther people lived from the equator, the lighter their skin tone was.

We have all evolved with different skin tones because of the area and climate our ancestors came from, but regardless of how much melanin we have, we are all one race. How did we get to a place where we compete and struggle to get along?

Do some research online to learn how the region your ancestors are from has affected your physical characteristics.

In the 1930s, the modern idea of "race" was introduced by the National Party in Germany. The party, called the Nazis, believed there was a master race of people that was superior to everyone else. This race was made up of people descended from Scandinavian and German warriors. Anyone whose relatives weren't White with roots in Scandinavian countries or Germany was unwanted.

People who didn't belong to the "master race" were killed during the Holocaust. No one knows just how many people died, but recent estimates are as high as 15 million to 20 million. Although everyone agrees that the Holocaust was bad, there are still people who believe that one "race" is superior to another.

Nazi Germany may be the most shameful example of racism, but the Germans were not alone. Long before they promoted the idea of a superior race, people were competing and fighting with others who looked or thought differently.

A respected Greek philosopher named Aristotle (384–322 BCE) wrote that some people were born to become masters while others were born to have masters. Aristotle's writings were popular for many centuries. The Europeans and the British used Aristotle's teachings as one way to justify taking over countries when people weren't Christians. This was called colonization.

The Europeans and the British also believed in making some people from those countries work for free. This was called enslavement. They kidnapped Black people from Africa and brought them to the American colonies in the 1600s and 1700s. The Africans were not Christians and were judged to be inferior—and were sold as slaves.

In the New World, colonists encountered the indigenous people of North America. We know these diverse groups as Native Americans. They too were not Christians and were considered inferior. Colonists killed and mistreated them to get the land we now call the United States.

Like the enslaved Africans, Native Americans' skin was darker than the colonists. The colonists eventually came to the conclusion that it was not only Christianity, but whiteness that made them superior. And so the concept of "race" was born on American soil.

Colonization had disastrous effects on indigenous populations, including war, disease, and enslavement.

Fighting RACISM in the Past

Racism has a long history, but so does anti-racism. Most anti-racists fight racism because they themselves have been treated unfairly. There are also supporters who help fight racism even though they don't experience it themselves.

In America's early years, when slavery was common, some enslaved people wanted their freedom so badly that they ran away. They ran even though they knew they would be beaten or killed if they were caught. They took dangerous paths to places where slavery was illegal. The network of secret routes that people traveled to freedom was called the Underground Railroad. People who helped others gain freedom were called abolitionists. There were many well-known Black abolitionists like Harriet Tubman and Frederick Douglass. There were also many White abolitionists who helped, like Harriet Beecher Stowe and John Brown. Abolitionists were early anti-racists.

Slavery finally ended in 1865 after the Northern states won a war against the Southern states. This was called the Civil War. Sadly, people who supported slavery still believed they were superior to the people they had enslaved. Southern states created laws to keep Black people from getting an education or good jobs. Southern laws and police officers would not protect Black people. Southern hospitals would not treat them. Restaurants and hotels in the South would not serve them.

Harriet Beecher Stowe wrote *Uncle Tom's Cabin*, a book that is sometimes noted as leading to the Civil War.

Black schools did not receive the same support or funding as White schools.

Without education, good jobs, or health care, Black people had to find ways to live a better life. They opened their own schools and colleges. They started their own banks and businesses, such as those in Harlem, New York, or on Black Wall Street in Tulsa, Oklahoma. Black people made their own movies and music. They started their own restaurants and sports leagues. They became doctors and teachers so they could take care of themselves and each other. Still, some things were harder to get, like the right to vote or own land. Black people realized that they had to pull together to stand up for their rights.

The most well-known anti-racism effort in the United States was the civil rights movement of the 1960s. These protests were well organized and had strong leaders who were able to convince all kinds of people to fight for change. The leaders were called activists.

Activists like Martin Luther King Jr., Malcolm X, and Amelia Boynton told Black people that the rights in the U.S. Constitution were meant for everyone. They convinced people to protest through rallies and marches. Most protests were peaceful, but not always. Sometimes the protests turned violent because protesters were hurt and angry at not being treated equally for such a long time. Sometimes protests turned violent because the police and White citizens were angry about Black people standing up for themselves. When people around the country saw protesters being attacked, some of them started showing support for Black people's struggle against racism.

Protests were only one way to fight racism. Some people became important "firsts" during this time. People like Ruby Bridges and the "Little Rock Nine" contended with threats and violence to become the first Black students to attend all-White schools in the South.

Others, like Barbara Jordan and Thurgood Marshall, fought racism from within the system. Barbara Jordan overcame poverty to become the first Black female congresswoman. Thurgood Marshall became the first Black U.S. Supreme Court justice.

John Lewis chose multiple paths to anti-racism. He helped Martin Luther King Jr. organize the March on Washington in 1963 and marched on "Bloody Sunday" in Selma, Alabama, in 1965. He became a six-term congressman before his death in 2020.

The civil rights movement was important because not only did Black people gain a lot of important rights, but also because laws were changed. These laws opened doors for other groups facing discrimination.

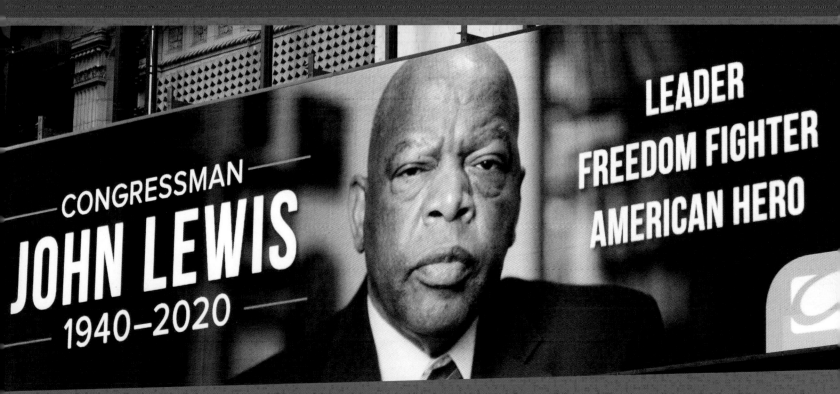

John Lewis Memorial in New York's Times Square.

ANTI-RACISM Today

The civil rights movement was responsible for many changes during the 1960s. Those changes did not stop racism, however. Black people and other people of color still have a harder time getting a good education. They have a harder time getting good jobs. They still have a hard time getting good health care. And they have a harder time in their encounters with police officers and the law.

There have been many legal battles and protests to help people continue to fight racism. Organizations like the National Association for the Advancement of Colored People (NAACP) and the Southern Christian Leadership Conference (SCLC) have remained strong, fighting racism behind the scenes.

Today, the Black Lives Matter movement is leading a new era in the fight for civil rights. Black Lives Matter began in 2013 as a hashtag started by three women, Alicia Garza, Patrisse Cullors, and Opal Tometi. The hashtag developed into a human rights organization that now advocates for social change.

The spring and summer of 2020 saw Black Lives Matter protests all around the world.

In May 2020, knowledge of the Black Lives Matter movement spread worldwide. George Floyd, a Black man in Minneapolis, Minnesota, was killed by a police officer. People who witnessed the killing used their cell phones to document it. The videos shocked people and made them sad and angry. People began to realize that Black people are sometimes treated differently when they come into contact with the police. They used the hashtags #blm and #BlackLivesMatter to organize rallies to protest police violence and racism. The marches were first held in Minneapolis where Floyd died. But as the news of his murder spread, people began to protest all over the world.

Some people who joined the protests were from the Black community. They were especially sad because Floyd's murder reminded them of others who had died or were hurt because of bias and racism.

Some people who joined the protests were not from the Black community. These people are called *allies*. An ally understands that they benefit from unearned privileges based on their skin color. An ally wants to help people who do not have those privileges.

DOING My Part

Not everyone who wants to fight racism goes out to protest. Some people find other ways to be anti-racist. They might write articles or books. They might organize social media campaigns. Others may donate to organizations that help people affected by racism. Still others talk with friends and family about how to support people who are mistreated because of their skin color.

There is no one way to fight racism. Fighting racism can be loud, like when you chant together at a rally. It can be quiet, like when you whisper to a friend that something they said is mean or racist. Sometimes, fighting racism can be completely silent, like following a hashtag or reading a book to learn how you can get better at being anti-racist.

One way you can be anti-racist at home is to talk with your family or friends about what you're learning and how you hope to be a part of positive change. Maybe you have learned things that your parents or grand-parents haven't learned. Even if they think differently about race than you do, that's okay. Maybe they will learn by watching you model being anti-racist.

At school, you can be anti-racist by standing up for people who are being treated differently because of how they look or identify. Standing up for someone can be as simple as not laughing at a racist joke or walking away from a crowd that's being mean. If you feel confident, you can even respectfully tell people engaging in racist behavior that they are being mean or hurtful.

You can be an activist at your school. You can get together with friends and form a group or club that hosts rallies or events that support anti-racism. You can start petitions with the help of a trusted adult on websites like Change.org. Or start your own podcast on Anchor.fm to talk about anti-racism and your values.

Together you can host a fund-raiser and donate to activist groups. You could even sign up with your parents and friends to march at an event in your area.

Even if no one around you thinks like you do, you can keep reading and learning. Websites like Tolerance.org and PBS.org have great anti-racist and historical articles. Smithsonian.org and YouTube have videos on many different Black history and anti-racist themes. Google searches for "Black history" and "anti-racism" will get you started. You can use your social media powers for good, sharing the content that you find.

Fannie Lou Hamer, a civil rights leader in the 1960s, said, "Nobody's free until everybody's free." Even if you aren't experiencing racism yourself, you can make the world a better place by helping others and becoming anti-racist in your own way.

What Is
WHITE PRIVILEGE?

What Does White
PRIVILEGE Look Like?

Imagine you're at the starting line of a race. Your heart is beating fast. You feel nervous as you wait to begin. You look up and down the starting line, sizing up the competition, wondering if you have enough speed to outrun them. Suddenly, an official steps into the middle of the track and tells the runners that obstacles will be placed in each person's lane. "Okay," you think, "that's kind of exciting." A crew of people come out with the obstacles.

As you look around, you notice that the obstacles being placed in the other runners' lanes look different than yours. You see high fences, large pools, mud, and barbed wire. In your lane, you see a row of hurdles that you've been taught to easily leap over. The other runners look confused. You are confused. How is it possible that your race will be so easy and their race will be so hard?

What you are experiencing in this moment is called privilege. Privilege is defined as a special right or advantage *granted* to one particular person or group. The word granted is an important part of the definition. Privilege is not something that is earned; it is *granted*, or given.

How is White privilege like a track race with unfair obstacles? How is it different?

There are a lot of different types of privilege that exist in society for a lot of different reasons. In the United States, racial bias and racism have led to something called White privilege. White privilege means that because of ongoing biases and racism in people and the places they work, White people have more access to power and resources than a Black, Indigenous, or Person of Color (BIPOC) in the same situation.

What are some things that may make it easier for White students to attend and finish college?

The phrase "in the same situation" is very important. For example, a White upper-class middle school student living in New York City will usually have more access to power and privileges than a Black upper-class middle school student. What do some of these powers and privileges look like? Books that these students read feature mostly White characters. (Around three-quarters of all children's books published in 2018 were about White people.) Students learn U.S. history from the perspective of White people. (A study by the Southern Poverty Law Center found that only 8 percent of graduating seniors believed that slavery was a main cause of the Civil War. It was.) White students are also more likely to be placed in advanced classes and are less likely to be suspended or arrested in school. Those things can make a big difference in people's lives!

Did you know that a Black boy who grows up in a wealthy community has a much greater chance of living in poverty as an adult than a White boy does? That Black boy may be just as smart and talented and may work just as hard as his White friend, but the Black boy may have more obstacles in his path that make gaining wealth more difficult. He may face racial discrimination when he tries to purchase a home or apply for a job. His White friend may have to overcome obstacles, but they will not involve racial discrimination, which means his friend has White privilege.

Sometimes, to understand what White privilege *is*, it's helpful to understand what White privilege is not. White privilege does not mean that White people have never worked hard. It does not mean that White people have not earned some of the success and power they have. It also does not mean White people have never suffered.

Think about this story. My great-grandfather was White and a coal miner in the 1920s. He worked long hours in the mines, earned very little money for his family, and suffered a lot. He got very sick from breathing in coal dust. The good news is, he also had the opportunity to work his way up to higher-paying jobs in the mines, build his own home, and raise a family.

Life for Black coal miners was usually different because of racism, discrimination, and few laws to protect them. The majority of Black coal miners worked the hardest and most dangerous jobs in the mines and received the lowest pay. All of this put more obstacles in place, preventing them from living a prosperous life. My great-grandfather worked hard and also benefited from his White privilege.

White privilege hurts a lot of people. If you are Black, you might have experienced this hurt, and it might make you angry or sad. If you are White, you might feel bad about hurting others or you might feel afraid to lose this privilege. You feel these things because White privilege is bad for everyone, including White people. That's because White privilege is the result of centuries of racism and bias.

There is hope! By learning more about White privilege, we can work to spend it, end it, and build a country where everyone has the opportunity to run—free of unfair obstacles and to the best of their ability.

President Lyndon Baines Johnson signing the Civil Rights Bill, April 11, 1968.

Where Did White PRIVILEGE come From?

Now you might be thinking, "Hey, wait a minute, doesn't everybody in the United States have the same opportunities? When slavery ended, didn't Black people become totally free?" Thinking this is technically right, but there are a lot of ways Black people have been prevented from accessing these rights. To understand a little better, let's travel back in time to an era called Reconstruction (1865–1877). During this period, attempts were made to fix inequalities caused by racism and slavery.

When slavery ended, three amendments were added to the U.S. Constitution giving Black people the same rights as White people. The 13th Amendment ended slavery. The 14th Amendment gave Black people the right to be an American citizen. The 15th Amendment gave Black men the right to vote. Black people also could now earn a paycheck, own land, and receive an education. For a little while, this worked. In fact, during Reconstruction, 1,500 Black leaders were voted into power. Some Black families that had been broken up because of slavery were reunited, and Black people began building free lives across America.

A family stands in front of the former slave quarters of the Hermitage Plantation, Savannah, Georgia, 1907.

Tragically, many White people, who had spent centuries enslaving Black people, did not like the power that Black people now had. These White people tried to take that power away. One organization that did this was the Ku Klux Klan. This hate group, which still exists, formed after the Civil War. It used violence to force Black people from their homes and jobs and to prevent them from voting. Reconstruction ended with the U.S. government unable to protect the rights of formerly enslaved people. Beginning in the 1870s and lasting until the 1960s, strict Jim Crow laws made segregation legal. This made it harder to get jobs, houses, and an education. It was a violent era. In fact, between 1882 and 1968, there were nearly 5,000 recorded lynchings of Black people in the United States, and many more lynchings likely went unrecorded. Many call this an era of racial terror.

Laws passed during the civil rights movement ended legal segregation in the 1960s. However, a lot of White people in power didn't want to follow the laws that were passed. When the United States passed a law saying that Black and White children must be allowed to go to the same public school, some states closed all of their public schools. White students in these states got money to go to private schools, and Black students were left without a school for several years.

You might be asking yourself, "Why would White people do this?" The answer lies in understanding what racism is. When the United States became a country, the people in charge had to create laws for its citizens. The people in charge were White, and most of them believed that Black people should be enslaved. They believed that Black people didn't deserve the same rights and freedoms as White people because they didn't see Black people as their equals. This is racial bias. This belief came from many places, including inaccurate descriptions of Africans and African culture from people who had traveled to the continent. And it came from a desire by White people to build wealth using the free labor that enslaved people provided.

Racism happens when racial bias leads to action. The actions that the people who founded this country took and the laws that they created deeply hurt people who were not White. That hurt continues today. White privilege and the advantages that come with it are the result of racial bias and racism.

The end of school segregation was an important milestone in the civil rights movement.

It's important to remember that White privilege is not the end of the story for Black people. Black people have not just walked away from the starting line because they looked down at their lane and saw the obstacles in their way. Throughout history, Black people have powerfully resisted racism, bias, and White privilege, and have overcome many obstacles. At the end of Reconstruction, Black people lost their homes and their jobs, so they built their own towns! The Jim Crow era was violent and unfair, so some Black people moved north to search for a better life. Some stayed in the South and fought to build their lives. When Black people saw how unfair segregation laws were, they stood against them and changed them during the civil rights movement.

Today, Black and White people around the nation see that things still aren't fair. Together, they are marching for new laws and more freedoms for BIPOC people in the United States and around the world!

Black Lives Matter protest in Breda, the Netherlands, 2020.

White PRIVILEGE Today

White privilege still exists today. It's easy to spot when you know some of the disparities in this country. In 2019, White workers who went to college earned over $10,000 more per year than Black workers who went to college. In 2016, schools with mostly White students received $23 billion (yes, you read that right) more per year than schools with mostly Black students. These kinds of differences give White people more power and more White privilege.

Hanging on to White privilege hurts BIPOC in the United States. Even though laws in our nation aren't overtly discriminatory, life is still not fair for BIPOC. Many laws are written with White privilege. This means that it will be easier for White people to follow the law and White people will get privileges because of the law.

Surrounding yourself with diverse friends will lead to a richer life.

For example, there is no law stating that police should arrest Black people more than White people. Yet Black people are more likely to be stopped, arrested, and killed by police officers than White people. This is true even though the same number of White and Black people commit crimes. When stopped and questioned by police, studies have shown that White people are more likely to receive the benefit of the doubt than Black people are. Black people may need others to back up what they say in order to be believed. These are examples of dangerous White privilege that many in our nation are trying to end.

Another example is school dress code policies. These rules about a person's appearance often impact a Black person's culture and style. For example, some schools say students can't wear dreadlocks or multiple barrettes in their hair. This rule affects Black students since they are more likely to wear their hair this way. One student, DeAndre Arnold, challenged this rule in his Texas school. DeAndre refused to cut his dreadlocks, explaining that his hair was part of his family's tradition. His family is from Trinidad. Many people believed that DeAndre should be allowed to keep his dreadlocks. His school, however, suspended him and would not allow him to attend his graduation.

This is an example of a rule that impacts Black students more than White students. And it's another example of White privilege.

These examples might make you feel discouraged, but don't give up hope. It is an exciting time! Many people are saying the laws and policies that create White privilege should be changed. Protests are happening around the country, and many organizations are asking for change. In schools, students are asking for new dress code policies, classes, and books that represent all people. White people who understand their privilege are using it to help remove obstacles that might prevent BIPOC from achieving success.

Taking ACTION

You might be wondering, "What can I do?" That is a very good question. If you are a student of color who is reading this, be encouraged. Look to your history and your community for ways to resist and stand against racism. Know your rights and learn how to use them. There may be obstacles in your path, but continue to work, like those who came before you, against those obstacles.

If you are a White person reading this, there are several steps you can take to end White privilege. First, understand that White privilege isn't good for anybody, even you! It does not feel good to have a lot of things that you didn't earn when other people don't get to have those same things. It does not feel good to see your Black friends or their families be less safe and have less opportunities than you do. When you are staring down that track, it might be exciting to think you're going to win the race because there are less obstacles in your way. But will you really feel good at the end of the race when you look back and see others fighting obstacles that you didn't even have? Instead of taking off down your path, what if you helped take away the obstacles in other runners' paths? Then they could join you in this great race of humanity.

Now that you know about White privilege, you can do something about it. Let's get working so we can all get running!

Pushing yourself to stand against White privilege can be uncomfortable, but it is essential for a more fair society.

What Is the BLACK LIVES MATTER MOVEMENT?

BLACK LIVES MATTER

Almost everyone is treated unfairly at some time in their life. People can be treated poorly because they belong to a certain cultural group or because of what they stand for. They can be discriminated against because of mental or physical disabilities. People can be treated unfairly because they are too rich or too poor, too tall or too short, too loud or too quiet, too religious or not religious enough.

But unfairness and anti-Black racism are different. America's legal and educational systems make it harder for people in the Black community to get a good education, be successful, and build wealth. When these systems put one cultural group at a disadvantage, it's called systemic racism.

Protesters rally toward the Sanford Police department in support of Trayvon Martin.

Black people are also subject to racial profiling. In 2012, Trayvon Martin was killed by a Neighborhood Watch volunteer. The Black teenager was unarmed and "looked suspicious." The shooter was charged with murder but found not guilty. This made people angry and sad. Alicia Garza, Patrisse Cullors, and Opal Tometi called for justice for Trayvon using the hashtag #BlackLivesMatter. The Black Lives Matter (BLM) movement was born the next year.

In 2014, another unarmed teenager, Michael Brown, was murdered by police in Ferguson, Missouri. Again, BLM responded, launching the organization into the mainstream as a movement. Since then, those advocating for justice in the deaths of other Black people have used the hashtag #BlackLivesMatter. The words "Black lives matter" are another way of saying, "Hey, the lives of Black people are important too!"

Signs in front of the White House show support for the Black Lives Matter movement in 2020.

BLM supports communities in their fight against anti-black racism. It also supports efforts by other marginalized groups—women's rights, LGBTQ (lesbian, gay, bisexual, transgender, and queer) rights, and immigrants' legal and human rights. Understanding the Black Lives Matter movement can help you support people who experience racism and the loss of human rights.

Bill De Blasio, Al Sharpton, and volunteers paint a Black Lives Matter mural on Fifth Avenue in New York City, in 2020.

BACKSTORY

Slavery in America started before the framing of the country's legal system. George Washington, James Madison, Benjamin Franklin, and others had enslaved people working in their homes cooking and cleaning. The enslaved Africans and their descendants worked the land of their enslavers to plant and harvest.

People rich enough to own people as slaves usually got richer because they kept the money they would have had to pay regular workers. The enslavers also had more rights and more privileges. People in slavery got nothing. They could not earn money. They could not inherit money from their fathers or pass money on to their children, which is how White families have been able to gain wealth across generations. For most of the Black people in America, especially in the South, enslavement continued for almost 250 years, from 1619 to 1865.

Once slaves were free, they lived in poverty and many died. If they survived, another 100 years of Jim Crow laws and segregation made America a difficult place for most former slaves and their descendants. These laws made it legal in many instances to prevent Black people from owning land or businesses.

Segregation was everywhere in American until the late 1900s.
Its effects are still felt today.

There were exceptions, like Harlem and Black Wall Street. These Black communities flourished with their own stores, banks, restaurants, luxury hotels, and fine homes. Black achievement drew many to these growing communities, but it also produced resentment in surrounding White communities. Black residents often faced violence and terrorism by White people, who beat and killed them and burned their homes and businesses to the ground.

Although slavery had ended, equal rights were not given to Black citizens. Especially in the South, segregation, violence, and lynching were used to maintain the pre–Civil War social order in which White people maintained power over Black people.

In 1921, violent mobs destroyed Black Wall Street.

To combat violence and discrimination, organizations like the NAACP were formed. Founded in 1909, the NAACP is the oldest, perhaps most well-known organization fighting for civil rights. Much like today's BLM movement, it began in response to riots in which Black people were targeted and killed. Most of the NAACP's early leadership was White and included women suffragists like Mary White Ovington and Inez Milholland.

Later in the 1900s, came the Congress of Racial Equality, the SCLC (led by Dr. Martin Luther King), and the Student Non-Violent Coordinating Committee (founded by Inez Baker).

These activist groups became the driving forces behind the great civil rights movement of the 1960s. Protests highlighted the systemic injustices still endured by Black people 100 years after the end of slavery. Activists led the Black community in advocating for human rights and for legal help and protections that had been historically denied them. Because of the civil rights movement, schools and businesses began to be integrated. Additionally, laws were made to protect Black people from vigilante and police violence.

BLM TODAY

After the protests of the 1960s, it seemed that there was real change in issues surrounding race in America. But data collected in the decades that followed showed racial progress in education and jobs had stalled or stopped.

Although the NAACP, SCLC, and other groups never stopped advocating for change, the number of large demonstrations and marches decreased until the 2000s. A number of high-profile killings of Black citizens in police custody and by White vigilantes showed that there was a renewed need for organized protests and anti-racist activism.

Massive crowds on Sunset Boulevard during Black Lives Matter protests. Los Angeles, June 14, 2020.

Patrisse Cullors grew up understanding the importance of powerful organizations like the NAACP and the National Action Network. But she didn't feel they were speaking to her generation. With well-known female and LGBTQ leaders, Black Lives Matter speaks to younger citizens. The movement is guided by an alliance of 16 local chapters that have the freedom to act in their communities. BLM's focus is on community action and social justice in the form of the following:

- Directing funding formerly dedicated to policing into educational and community programming.

- Expanding investment in Black business, health care, education, and community ventures to make up for the years Black citizens were kept from accessing and building wealth.

- Ending unfair practices like gerrymandering and voter supression.

The Black Lives Matter movement gained international support when George Floyd was killed by a police officer in 2020. BLM protests began in Minneapolis, where Floyd was murdered, and quickly spread throughout the country. Most major U.S. cities held rallies and marches.

The horrific images of Floyd's murder went viral, and the movement became one of the largest in history. People around the world began to advocate for anti-racist policing and human rights for Black American citizens. They examined racism in their own countries. BLM marches, rallies, and vigils were held in over 60 countries and on every continent except Antarctica. Protests were held in streets, town squares, and in front of U.S. embassies.

Some governments—like those in Fort Worth, Texas, and Washington, D.C.—allowed citizens to paint "Black Lives Matter" on certain streets. The murals, in bold yellow and black letters, cover several city blocks. The mural in Washington, D.C., is near the White House and is large enough to be seen from space.

In the spring, summer, and fall of 2020, an estimated 20 million people protested in support of Black Lives Matter.

In keeping with the movement's values, almost all of the protests worldwide were peaceful. However, some of the protesters were not members of the movement and did not have the same values. Fringe groups looted and vandalized property.

Military veterans holding a sign and American flag in support of Black lives and First Amendment rights.

Aerial shot of a Black Lives Matter mural on Fulton Street in Brooklyn, New York. It is 375 feet (114.3 meters) wide, and the letters are 28 feet (8.5 m) tall.

Some media outlets began to focus on violent clashes between citizens and police. Propaganda on social media blamed Black Lives Matter for the violence. Some people wrongly believed that BLM thought only Black lives mattered. They condemned BLM as violent and anti-White. These groups, some with ties to White supremacist groups, started using hashtags like #AllLivesMatter and #BlueLivesMatter.

Tweets by U.S. President Donald Trump also spread anti-BLM sentiment, calling the movement a "symbol of hate." Social media posts and misinformation further inflamed tensions.

Federal troops were sent into some cities to crack down on local protesters. Violent clashes worsened.

Anti-racist groups like #WallofMoms and #WallofVets came out in support of BLM. These largely White groups protested the presence of federal troops and police violence. Local governments filed lawsuits against the U.S. government for violating First Amendment rights. The United Nations and Amnesty International, two government watchdogs, issued human rights violation warnings to the U.S. government because citizens and journalists were being harmed and jailed.

Federal troops were withdrawn, but negative media coverage hurt the Black Lives Matter image. Leaders of the movement condemned violence, breaking with groups that weren't focused solely on the issues. Calls for peace and focus on the movement's message have followed.

When using social media and reading online news, be sure you know the information is from a credible source before believing or sharing it.

SUPPORTI G BLM

There are many ways to support the Black Lives Matter movement. Some people march. Some promote content highlighting the ongoing need for social change on social media. Others help paint murals like the ones pictured in this book. Some people donate to the Black Lives Matter Global Foundation to help fund advocacy groups. Still others support the movement's core values by standing up for Black people or anyone being treated unfairly because of how they look or identify.

Supporting and valuing the lives of Black citizens is supporting and valuing human life. Valuing human life is what Black Lives Matter is all about.

About the Authors

Hedreich Nichols, author, educator, and host of the YouTube series on equity #SmallBites, is a retired Grammy-nominated singer-songwriter turned EdTech teacher who uses her experience as a "one Black friend" to help others understand race, equity, and how to celebrate diversity. When not educating and advocating, she enjoys making music with her son, multi-instrumentalist @SwissChrisOnBass.

Leigh Ann Erickson has taught in New York City, Chicago, rural Ohio, and Mt. Vernon, Iowa. She aims to eradicate racism through justice driven curriculum. Erickson is founder of Undone Consulting and The Undone Movement, a nationwide movement of racial reconciling. Grateful to play a small role in centuries long resistance work, she owes much to her family, friends, and mentors.

Kelisa Wing honorably served in the U.S. Army and has been an educator for 14 years. She is the author of *Promises and Possibilities: Dismantling the School to Prison Pipeline, If I Could: Lessons for Navigating an Unjust World*, and *Weeds & Seeds: How to Stay Positive in the Midst of Life's Storms*. She speaks both nationally and internationally about discipline reform, equity, and student engagement. Kelisa lives in Northern Virginia with her husband and two children.